The Canterville Ghost

Oscar **Wilde**

Illustrated by **Paolo D'Altan**

Text adaptation and activities by **Gina D. B. Clemen**

Series editor : Robert Hill
Editor : Maria Gabriella Canelli, Sara Servente
Design and art direction : Nadia Maestri
Computer graphics : Carlo Cibrario-Sent, Simona Corniola
Picture research : Alice Graziotin

© 2015 Black Cat

First edition : January 2015

DeA Scuola, DeA Live, DeArte, DeA Events, DeA Formazione, DeA Link,
Deaflix are trademarks licensed by De Agostini Editore SpA

Picture credits : Dreamstime; Istockphoto; Shutterstock; Thinkstock; DeAgostini
Picture Library: 4; The Princes Edward and Richard in the Tower, 1878 (oil on canvas),
Millais, Sir John Everett (1829-96) / Royal Holloway, University of London /
Bridgeman Images: 21; DeAgostini Picture Library:22; MJ Kim/Getty Images: 23;
Universal History Archive/UIG/ Getty Images: 51t; Museum of London/Heritage
Images/Getty Images: b; DeAgostini Picture Library:52bc,75; Courtesy Everett
Collection/Contrasto: 77.

We would be happy to receive your comments and suggestions, and give you any
other information concerning our material.
info@blackcat-cideb.com
blackcat-cideb.com

Member of CISQ Federation

RINA
ISO 9001:2008
Certified Quality System

The design, production and distribution of educational materials
for the Black Cat brand are managed in compliance with the rules of
Quality Management System which fulfils the requirements of the
standard ISO 9001 (Rina Cert. No. 24298/02/S - IQNet Reg. No. IT-80096)

Printed in Italy by Litoprint, Genoa

Contents

The text is recorded in full.

 These symbols indicate the beginning and end of the passages
linked to the listening activities.

Oscar Wilde

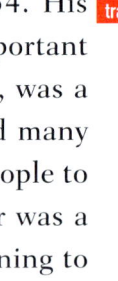

track 02

Oscar Wilde was born in Dublin, Ireland, on 16 October 1854. His father, William, was an important doctor and his mother, Jane, was a poet. Oscar's parents invited many interesting and important people to their home in Dublin. Oscar was a young boy and he liked listening to them.

When he completed his education in Ireland, he studied at Oxford University in England. He was an excellent student and won prizes for his poetry. He was funny and clever, and people liked listening to him. He liked to be the centre of attention and had unusual ideas about art and life. He loved beautiful things and wore unusual clothes. In 1879 Oscar Wilde went to live in London and he began writing. In 1882 he went to the United States of America to talk to audiences in different cities about his writing. Many Americans went to listen to him. In 1884 he married Constance Lloyd and had two sons.

He wrote his most famous children's story, 'The Happy Prince', for his sons. He wrote poems, short stories, plays for the theatre and one novel. He was very popular and everyone invited him to their dinner parties.

Wilde published *The Canterville Ghost* in 1887.

Two of his most famous works are his novel, *The Picture of Dorian Gray* and his play, *The Importance of Being Earnest*.

Oscar Wilde died in 1900.

1 COMPREHENSION CHECK

Are the following sentences true (T) or false (F)? Correct the false ones.

		T	F
1	Oscar Wilde was born in Oxford, England.	☐	☐
2	Oscar's parents were important people.	☐	☐
3	He was a clever man but not a good student.	☐	☐
4	Americans were not interested in Oscar Wilde.	☐	☐
5	In London he became a famous writer.	☐	☐
6	"The Happy Prince" was a story for his two sons.	☐	☐

2 DISCUSSION

In your country, is there any artist – writer, poet, musician, painter - who is unusual and interesting? Why is this person unusual and interesting?

3 WHAT DO YOU KNOW ABOUT GHOSTS?

A Take this quiz and find out! For each sentence choose either true (T) or false (F).

		T	F
1	Ghosts can move through walls.	☐	☐
2	You can never see ghosts because they're invisible.	☐	☐
3	Some ghosts are bad.	☐	☐
4	Ghosts only live in haunted [1] houses.	☐	☐
5	When you see a ghost your watch stops.	☐	☐
6	Ghosts always carry their heads in their hands.	☐	☐
7	Ghosts can't talk.	☐	☐

B Now answer these questions.

1 Work with your partner and describe a ghost.
2 Now draw a picture of a ghost.
3 Compare your answers and pictures with your classmates.

1. **haunted** : a place with ghosts.

From left to right: **Mr Hiram Otis, Mrs Lucretia Otis,
Washington Otis, Virginia Otis, Mrs Umney, the Otis twins,
Cecil, Lord Canterville, the Canterville Ghost.**

BEFORE YOU READ

1 **VOCABULARY**
Match the words with their meaning. Use a dictionary if necessary.

1 ☐ haunted   **3** ☐ twins
2 ☐ frightened   **4** ☐ the Stars and Stripes

2 **LISTENING**
🔊 **Listen to Chapter One and choose the correct answer – A, B or C.**

track 03

1 Mr Otis was an American

A ☐ who wanted to buy Canterville Chase.

B ☐ who wanted to sell Canterville Chase to an English lord.

C ☐ who wanted to go back to America.

2 The Canterville family

A ☐ lived in London.

B ☐ was going to America.

C ☐ didn't want to live in a haunted house.

3 Mrs Otis

A ☐ was a minister of the United States Government.

B ☐ had four children.

C ☐ was afraid of ghosts.

4 'The Stars and Stripes'

A ☐ were twins.

B ☐ liked dancing.

C ☐ liked riding their pony in the country.

CHAPTER ONE

Canterville Chase

M r Hiram B. Otis was American. He was rich and important. He wanted to live in an old house in England so he decided to buy Canterville Chase. Everyone told him that he was very stupid because Canterville Chase was haunted.

Lord Canterville was the owner of Canterville Chase and said to Mr Otis, 'I don't live in this house because it's haunted. Members of my family saw the ghost many times. They were terribly frightened. My wife, Lady Canterville, can't sleep here at night because there are strange noises in the house.'

'My Lord,' said Mr Otis, 'I'll buy the house with the furniture and the ghost. I come from a modern country and we have everything that money can buy. If there are ghosts in Europe, an American will probably take one back home. He'll put it in a museum for everyone to see.'

Lord Canterville smiled and said, 'There's a ghost in this house and it always appears before someone in the family dies.'

Canterville Ghost

'Well,' said Mr Otis, laughing, 'in my home the *doctor* appears before someone in the family dies. But I'm an American and we don't believe in ghosts. They're an old European idea.'

'If you don't mind a ghost in the house, that's alright,' said Lord Canterville. 'But please remember that I told you.'

A few weeks later Lord Canterville sold Canterville Chase to the Americans.

There were six people in the Otis family. Mr Otis was a minister [1] of the United States Government.

His wife, Mrs Lucretia Otis, was a beautiful woman. When she was a young lady in New York City, she was famous for her beauty. She was healthy and strong.

Washington was the oldest son of the family. His parents called him Washington, because the first president of the United States was called George Washington. He was tall and good-looking, and had blond hair. He liked dancing very much and liked living in Great Britain.

Virginia Otis was fifteen years old and she was lovely. She had blonde hair and big blue eyes. She loved riding her pony in the country. A young English lord, Cecil, Duke of Cheshire, liked her very much.

The youngest children were twins. They were often called 'the Stars and Stripes', like the name that people called the American flag. They were often naughty [2] but everyone liked them.

---

1. **minister** : An important person who works for the government of a country.
2. **naughty** : When you don't behave well.

UNDERSTANDING THE TEXT

1 COMPREHENSION CHECK

Are these sentences 'Right' (A) or 'Wrong' (B)? If there is not enough information to answer 'Right' (A) or 'Wrong' (B), choose 'Doesn't Say' (C). There is an example at the beginning (0).

		A	B	C
0	Mr Otis was an important man who worked for the American government.	✓		
1	Mr Otis was tall and good-looking.			
2	Nobody told Mr Otis about the ghost at Canterville Chase.			
3	Mr Otis decided to buy the house but not the old furniture.			
4	The Canterville ghost always appeared after a family member died.			
5	Mrs Lucretia Otis came from New York City.			
6	Mrs Lucretia Otis was thirty-six years old.			
7	Washington did not like living in Great Britain.			
8	The young Duke of Cheshire was Virginia's good friend.			
9	Virginia's pony was brown and white.			
10	'The Stars and Stripes' were the youngest children of the Otis family.			

T: GRADE 3

2 SPEAKING – WORK

Mr Otis is a minister of the American government. Talk with your partner about the job you want to do. Use these questions to help you.

1 What kind of job do you want to do?
2 Why do you want to do this job?
3 Is it easy, difficult, interesting, dangerous or boring?
4 What subjects do you need to study to do this job?
5 Do you know someone who does this job?

3 OPPOSITES

Match the word with its opposite.

1 ☐ clever   A new
2 ☐ buy   B short
3 ☐ old   C stupid
4 ☐ ugly   D sell
5 ☐ tall   E beautiful

4 AMERICAN AND BRITISH ENGLISH

A How different is American English from British English? Take this fun quiz and find out. Mark USA or UK for the words below.
Do you know the meaning of all the words?
Then write the correct synonym in the third column. There is an example at the beginning (0).

		UK	USA	SYNONYMS
0	Elevator	☐	✓	Lift
1	Post	☐	☐	....
2	Holiday	☐	☐	....
3	Mail	☐	☐	....
4	Petrol	☐	☐	....
5	Gas	☐	☐	....
6	Lift	☐	☐	....
7	Vacation	☐	☐	....

B There are spelling differences too. Words that end in –re in British English often end in –er in American English. And words that end in –our in British English often end in –or in American English.
Look at the examples below.

Words that end in –re

UK	USA
cent**re**	cent**er**
theat**re**	theat**er**

Words that end in –our

UK	USA
col**our**	col**or**
hum**our**	hum**or**

C Now find the 8 words from the table in part A in the word square. Circle the British words in red and the American words in blue.

```
C M S E J B D H G X A B M O
O R W I A U T U M N I N P H
M V E K G S U C L D C A E O
A D E L O H O G A S H G T L
I C T T E O F O T N E O R I
L B S P Z V G U N K D B O D
S O R A Y P A E D N R Y L A
P A N G S R F T G A F X Z Y
W K U M V A S D O I D A O A
V A C A T I O N F R U L L U
F X P U L I F T I K S V R L
```

SHE *LOVED* RIDING HER PONY IN THE COUNTRY.

We form the Past Simple of regular verbs by adding **–ed** to the verb.
*work - work**ed***   *help - help**ed***   *talk - talk**ed***

When the verb already ends in -e, add only **–d** to the verb.
*love - lov**ed***   *hate - hat**ed***   *complete - complet**ed***

Some verbs end in a **consonant + y**. We remove the 'y' and add **–ied**.
*study - stud**ied***   *carry - carr**ied***   *hurry - hurr**ied***

But if verbs end in a **vowel + y**, the 'y' does not change.
*play - play**ed***   *stay - stay**ed***   *enjoy - enjoy**ed***

5   THE PAST SIMPLE – REGULAR VERBS

A   Complete the following sentences with the Past Simple of the verbs given.

> appear   work   stay   like   want   study   play   hurry

1   Mr Otis .... to live in an old English house.
2   Washington and Virginia .... French at school.
3   The twins .... in the garden after school.
4   The ghost .... at midnight.
5   They .... home because it was very late.
6   Washington .... dancing.
7   Mr Otis .... for the American Government.
8   The children .... home because it was raining.

B   Unscramble the verbs below and then put them in the crossword in the Past Simple form.

Down

1   okol   ....
2   phle   ....
3   msile   ....

Across

4   altk   ....
5   cdeied   ....

6   DISCUSSION

Work with your partner and make two lists. Then present them to the class.

1   What British and American foods do you know?
2   What American and British singers and bands do you know?

BEFORE YOU READ

1 VOCABULARY

A Match each word with the right picture.

1 ☐ Hall   3 ☐ Stain   5 ☐ Flash of
2 ☐ Fireplace   4 ☐ Carriage   lightning

B Match each word with the right definition.

1 ☐ Housekeeper   A Very terrible.
2 ☐ Blood   B A person who looks after the house.
3 ☐ Horrible   C A loud noise in the sky when there is a storm.
4 ☐ Thunder   D Red liquid that flows around our body.

2 LISTENING

track 04

Listen to Chapter Two and choose the correct answer – A, B or C.

1 The Otis family arrived at Canterville Chase
   A ☐ in June.
   B ☐ in July.
   C ☐ in January.

2 The weather at Canterville Chase was
   A ☐ rainy and cloudy.
   B ☐ very windy.
   C ☐ lovely.

3 Mrs Umney was
   A ☐ the owner of Canterville Chase.
   B ☐ the ghost of Canterville Chase.
   C ☐ the housekeeper at Canterville Chase.

4 There was a bloodstain
   A ☐ on the floor of the library.
   B ☐ on the floor of the hall.
   C ☐ in Mrs Otis's bedroom.

CHAPTER TWO

The Stain

Canterville Chase was seven miles [1] from the town of Ascot. When the family came to live at Canterville Chase, they drove from the train station in a carriage. It was a lovely July evening. But as they came near Canterville Chase, the weather changed. Dark clouds appeared [2] in the sky. Some big black birds flew over their heads. It began to rain.

track 04

An old woman dressed in black was waiting for them on the steps of the house. This was Mrs Umney, the housekeeper.

'Welcome to Canterville Chase,' she said. The Otis family followed her through the dark hall into the library. Suddenly Mrs Otis saw a dark red stain on the floor near the fireplace.

'What's that stain?' she asked.

'It's blood,' answered Mrs Umney.

---

1. **seven miles** : about 10 km.
2. **appeared** : when someone or something appears, you can see it.

'How horrible!' cried Mrs Otis. 'I don't want bloodstains in the library. Please clean it.'

Mrs Umney smiled and said in a low, mysterious voice, 'It's the blood of Lady Eleanore de Canterville. Her husband, Sir Simon de Canterville, killed her there in 1575. Sir Simon disappeared [3] nine years later and no one found his body. But his ghost still haunts Canterville Chase. And no one can clean the stain.'

'What nonsense!' cried Washington in a loud voice. '"Pinkerton's Champion Cleaner" will clean it. It cleans *everything*!'

He took the 'Pinkerton's Champion Cleaner' from his suitcase and cleaned the stain with it. In a few minutes the stain disappeared.

'Look!' he said happily, 'the stain's gone! "Pinkerton's" is the best!'

Suddenly there was a great flash of lightning and then thunder. Everyone jumped up and Mrs Umney fainted. [4]

'What terrible weather!' said Mr Otis calmly.

'Hiram, look at Mrs Umney,' said Mrs Otis, 'she fainted. What can we do with her?'

'We'll pay her less,' said Mr Otis.

When Mrs Umney heard this she got up and felt better. But she was very worried.

'Mr Otis, please don't laugh at the ghost,' said Mrs Umney. 'Terrible things happen in this house. I often can't sleep at night because the ghost makes strange noises.'

'Mrs Umney,' said Mr Otis calmly, 'don't worry. My wife and I are not afraid of ghosts.'

'Very well, sir,' said the old housekeeper. 'Good night!'

---

3. **disappeared** : when someone or something disappears, you can't see it any more.
4. **fainted** : fell on the floor and lost consciousness.

UNDERSTANDING THE TEXT

1 COMPREHENSION CHECK

Match each sentence (1-7) to its correct ending (A-G) to make a summary of Chapter Two.

1 ☐ The Otis family arrived at Canterville Chase
2 ☐ When the family came near Canterville Chase
3 ☐ Mrs Umney
4 ☐ Sir Simon de Canterville
5 ☐ Washington cleaned the stain
6 ☐ Mrs Umney could not sleep well

A welcomed the family to Canterville Chase.
B because the ghost made strange noises.
D in the month of July.
E with 'Pinkerton's Champion Cleaner'.
F the weather changed there and it began to rain.
G killed his wife in the library in 1575.

2 THE WEATHER

Look at the pictures and fill in the gaps. Use the words in the box below.

| sunny | snowing | icy | windy | raining | foggy |

1 It's ....y.   **2** It's ....y.   **3** It's ....y.

4 It's .... ing.   **5** It's .... ing.   **6** It's ....y.

3 SPEAKING – THE WEATHER

It was a stormy evening at Canterville Chase when the Otis family got there. Talk to your partner about the weather. Use these questions to help you.

1 What's the weather like where you live?
2 What is your favourite kind of weather and why?
3 What is winter like in your area?
4 Do you play winter sports?
5 What do you do when the weather is very hot?
6 What's the weather like today?

SOME BIG BLACK BIRDS *FLEW* OVER THEIR HEADS. IT *BEGAN* TO RAIN.

Some verbs have irregular Past Simple forms: **flew** (fly) and **began** (begin).
Here are some other examples

	Past Simple		Past Simple
be	was, were	think	thought
go	went	eat	ate
come	came	leave	left

4 THE PAST SIMPLE: IRREGULAR VERBS

Complete the table with the Past Simple form of the verbs below.
All the verbs are in the first two chapters of the story.

	Past Simple		Past Simple
say		see	
sell		hear	
tell		begin	
do		feel	
drive		get	
fly		take	

Edward and Richard in the Tower, by Sir John Everett Millais, 1878.

Famous Ghosts

What is a ghost?

track 05

Centuries ago people talked about ghosts and spirits, and they still talk about them today. But no one knows exactly what a ghost is! Some scientists study ghosts and haunted places. They try to understand strange events of the past and present. Others try to photograph ghosts and sometimes ghosts appear in photographs — but no one can explain why.

So what is a ghost? The most common explanation is this: ghosts are spirits of the dead. They died in a terrible way and they haunt the place where they died. It can be a house, a castle, a theatre, a forest, a road or a ship. They cannot rest in peace.

There are good ghosts and bad ghosts. In Great Britain people say there are a lot of haunted places.

Royal Ghosts

Glamis Castle in Scotland is a big castle with more than one hundred rooms. It has a long history of ghosts, strange noises and terrible secrets. The Tower of London is a popular attraction and many people think it is haunted by royal ghosts. The most famous ghosts of the Tower are two young princes, Edward and Richard. In 1483 Edward V became King of England and he was only twelve years old. His brother Richard was ten. Their uncle, Richard, Duke of Gloucester, wanted to be King of

England so he killed the two princes in the Tower. He then became King Richard III.

In 1674 workmen found the skeletons [1] of two children under the stairs of the Tower. Some people see the two ghosts of the young princes at the bottom of the stairs.

Anne Boleyn is another royal ghost who haunts the Tower of London. She was King Henry VIII's second wife, but she did not give him a son. In 1536 King Henry decided to marry another woman. Anne Boleyn was beheaded [2] in the Tower in May 1536.

Another haunted place is Hampton Court Palace, near London. Catherine Howard was King Henry VIII's fifth wife and she was beheaded there in 1542. People say that her ghost haunts Hampton Court Palace.

A portrait of Anne Boleyn by an unknown artist, 1533-1536.

Ghosts in Literature

Ghosts are part of literature. William Shakespeare wrote about ghosts in several of his plays. In *Hamlet* the castle guards see the ghost of Hamlet's father one night. Then the ghost speaks to his son, Hamlet, and tells him terrible things about his murder. Shakespeare's play *Macbeth* begins with three old witches. They tell Macbeth and his friend Banquo strange things about their future. After Banquo's death, his ghost appears at the dinner table and frightens Macbeth.

Charles Dickens's *A Christmas Carol* (1843) is a famous ghost story with four ghosts. The first ghost is Scrooge's business partner, Jacob Marley, who is now dead. The others are the ghosts of Christmas Past, Christmas Present and Christmas Yet to Come. It is a wonderful ghost story with a very happy ending.

The American writers Nathaniel Hawthorne, Edgar Allan Poe and Henry James wrote about good and bad ghosts and spirits in their stories.

1. **Skeleton** :    2. **beheaded** : her head was cut off.

Stage version of Dickens's *A Christmas Carol*, London Palladium, 2005.

1 COMPREHENSION CHECK

Are the following sentences true (T) or false (F)? Correct the false ones.

T F

1 Ghosts never appear in photographs.

2 Most ghosts are bad.

3 Glamis Castle is a haunted place.

4 Two young princes haunt the Tower of London.

5 Anne Boleyn haunts Hampton Court Palace.

6 Catherine Howard was beheaded in the Tower of London.

7 In Shakespeare's play, Hamlet's father was a ghost.

8 Charles Dickens wrote a famous ghost story.

9 American writers wrote about bad ghosts.

2 DISCUSSION

1 Do you know any ghost stories from your country?

2 Are there any haunted places in the town or city where you live?

BEFORE YOU READ

1 **VOCABULARY**

Match the words with their meaning. Use a dictionary if necessary.

1 wrist   **2** ankle   **3** chain   **4** 'Rising Sun American Lubricator'

A

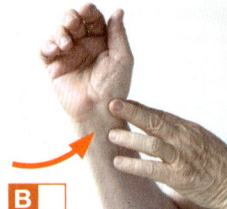
B

C

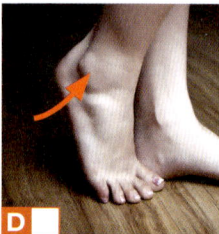
D

2 **LISTENING**

Listen to Chapter Three and and choose the correct answer – A, B or C.

track 06

1 During the night
- A ☐ there was a big storm.
- B ☐ there was a lot of wind.
- C ☐ there was a lot of noise in the garden.

2 Mr Otis kept the key to the library door
- A ☐ in his bedroom.
- B ☐ in his hand.
- C ☐ in his pocket.

3 Everyone went to bed
- A ☐ at ten o'clock.
- B ☐ at half past eleven.
- C ☐ at eleven.

4 The ghost's chains were
- A ☐ heavy.
- B ☐ noisy.
- C ☐ black.

3 **READING PICTURES**

Look at the picture on page 27 and answer the questions.

1 What is Mr Otis doing?
2 What is the name on the label of the bottle?
3 Describe the ghost.

CHAPTER THREE

The Ghost Appears

There was a terrible storm all night. The next morning when the Otis family came downstairs to breakfast the stain was there again. Washington was surprised and unhappy.

'I don't understand what happened,' said Washington. '"Pinkerton's Champion Cleaner" always works.'

He cleaned the floor with 'Pinkerton's Champion Cleaner' and the stain disappeared. But the next morning the stain was there again. Washington cleaned the floor for the third time. His father closed the library door that night and kept the key in his pocket. But in the morning the stain was still there.

'This is interesting,' said Mr Otis. 'Perhaps the house really is haunted.'

That evening the Otis family went for a ride and returned home at nine o'clock for dinner. During the ride they talked about the things important Americans always talk about.

'American actors are better than European actors,' said Mr Otis.

'American food is better than English food,' said Mrs Otis.

'The city of Boston is more important than Rome,' said Washington.

'American boys are taller than English boys,' said the twins, smiling.

No one in the Otis family talked about Sir Simon de Canterville. But that night they discovered that there *was* a ghost at Canterville Chase.

At eleven o'clock everyone went to bed. Some time later Mr Otis woke up because he heard a strange noise outside his room. He looked at the clock. It was one o'clock. He opened his bedroom door.

In front of him there was a terrible old man. His eyes were red like fire. His long grey hair was dirty. His clothes were very old. On his wrists and ankles there were heavy chains.

Mr Otis looked at him calmly and said, 'My dear sir, your chains are making a terrible noise. You'll wake up everyone in the house. Take this bottle of "Rising Sun American Lubricator". Put it on your chains and they won't make noise any more.'

Mr Otis put the bottle of "Rising Sun American Lubricator" on the table outside his bedroom and went back to bed.

The ghost was very surprised. He took the bottle and threw it on the floor angrily. Then he ran down the hall and made terrible sounds. Suddenly another bedroom door opened and the twins appeared. They threw their big white pillows at him. The ghost of Sir Simon de Canterville disappeared through the wall into his secret room.

'For three hundred years I frightened everyone in this house,' he thought. 'Famous lords shot themselves [1] and famous ladies drowned themselves [2] in the lake. Servants always ran away. After all of my success, these modern Americans come here and have no respect [3] for me. This is horrible! I must do something.'

---

1. **shot themselves** : killed themselves with a gun.
2. **drowned themselves** : killed themselves in the water.
3. **respect** : if you respect a person you have a good opinion of him/her and you are polite.

UNDERSTANDING THE TEXT

1 **KEY** **COMPREHENSION CHECK**

**Read these sentences about Chapter Three. Choose the correct answer –
A, B or C. There is an example at the beginning (0).**

0 Washington was very unhappy

A ☑ because the stain was there again.

B ☐ because he didn't like living at Canterville Chase.

C ☐ because he lost the key to the library.

1 During their ride the Otis family

A ☐ sang an American song.

B ☐ talked about Mrs Umney.

C ☐ talked about the things important Americans always talk about.

2 Mr Otis said that

A ☐ American actors were better than European actors.

B ☐ American actors were taller than European actors.

C ☐ European actors were better than American actors.

3 At one o'clock in the morning Mr Otis

A ☐ went to bed because he was very tired.

B ☐ woke up because he heard a strange noise.

C ☐ went downstairs to the library.

4 Mr Otis told the ghost

A ☐ to go back to bed.

B ☐ to change his old clothes.

C ☐ to use a special product for his noisy chains.

5 The ghost was very angry

A ☐ because the Americans were not afraid of him.

B ☐ because the Americans made a lot of noise at night.

C ☐ because his chains were too heavy for him.

6 The ghost frightened everyone in the house

A ☐ for 200 years.

B ☐ for 30 years.

C ☐ for 300 years.

2 CHARACTERS

Write a short description of each of the characters below. Use the words in the box. You can use the same words more than once.

old   terrible
young   healthy
rich   American
housekeeper   strong
tall   lovely
blue eyes   blond hair
naughty   important
good-looking
wears a black dress
likes dancing
frightening
likes riding a pony
killed his wife
long grey hair
minister of the United
States Government
beautiful   red eyes

3 PARTS OF THE BODY

Look at the picture of the girl and label the parts of the body with the words below. Use a dictionary if necessary.

1 Head
2 Nose
3 Eyes
4 Ears
5 Teeth
6 Mouth
7 Neck
8 Arm
9 Wrist
10 Hand
11 Fingers
12 Leg
13 Knee
14 Ankle
15 Foot

'AMERICAN BOYS ARE *TALLER* THAN ENGLISH BOYS,' SAID THE TWINS. 'THE CITY OF BOSTON IS *MORE IMPORTANT* THAN ROME,' SAID WASHINGTON.

Taller is the comparative form of 'tall'.

We form comparative adjectives like this:

- adjectives of one syllable, we add **–er** to the end of the adjective;

  *tall – tall**er***   *old – old**er***

- if the adjective is consonant-vowel-consonant, e.g. *hot*, we double the final consonant;

  *hot – hot**ter***   *big – big**ger***

- with adjectives of two syllables ending in **–y**, we remove the 'y' and add – **ier**;

  *easy – eas**ier***   *happy – happ**ier***

- with adjectives of two or more syllables, we use **more** before the adjective.

  *beautiful – **more** beautiful,*   *important – **more** important*

Be careful! Some adjective have an irregular comparative form.

  *good – **better***   *bad – **worse***

4   **COMPARATIVE ADJECTIVES**

Fill in the gaps with the correct comparative adjective.

1   The ice-cream was good but the chocolate cake was .... (*good*)

2   Canterville Chase is .... (*big*) than Mr Otis's American home.

3   Mr Otis is .... (*tall*) than his son Washington.

4   English winters are .... (*bad*) than California winters.

5   Riding a horse is .... (*difficult*) than riding a pony.

6   Virginia is .... (*pretty*) than her friends.

7   Mrs Otis is .... (*modern*) than Mrs Umney.

8   'My book is .... (*funny*) than yours,' said Virginia.

9   Summers in Boston are .... (*hot*) than summers in London.

10   'My clothes are .... (*beautiful*) than Mrs Umney's', said Virginia.

BEFORE YOU READ

1 VOCABULARY

Match the words with their meaning. Use a dictionary if necessary.

1 suit of armour   **2** bones   **3** peashooter   **4** candle

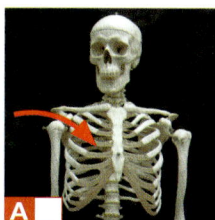 **A**
 **B**
 **C**
 **D**

2 LISTENING

Listen to Chapter Four and choose the correct answer – A, B or C.

1 The twins hit the ghost with
  A ☐ a bottle.
  B ☐ their shoes.
  C ☐ their pillows.

2 Washington cleaned the stain on the floor
  A ☐ every evening.
  B ☐ every morning.
  C ☐ once a week.

3 Every day the stain
  A ☐ got bigger.
  B ☐ got smaller.
  C ☐ changed colour.

4 Mrs Otis gave the ghost
  A ☐ a peashooter.
  B ☐ a bottle of medicine.
  C ☐ a suit of armour.

5 Sir Simon decided
  A ☐ to plan a revenge for the Otis famly.
  B ☐ to hide in his secret room forever.
  C ☐ to leave Canterville Chase.

3 READING PICTURES

Look at the picture on page 35 and answer the questions.

1 What is Mrs Otis doing?
2 Do you think Mrs Otis is afraid of the ghost? Why or why not?
3 In your opinion, how does the ghost feel?
4 What can you see on the floor?

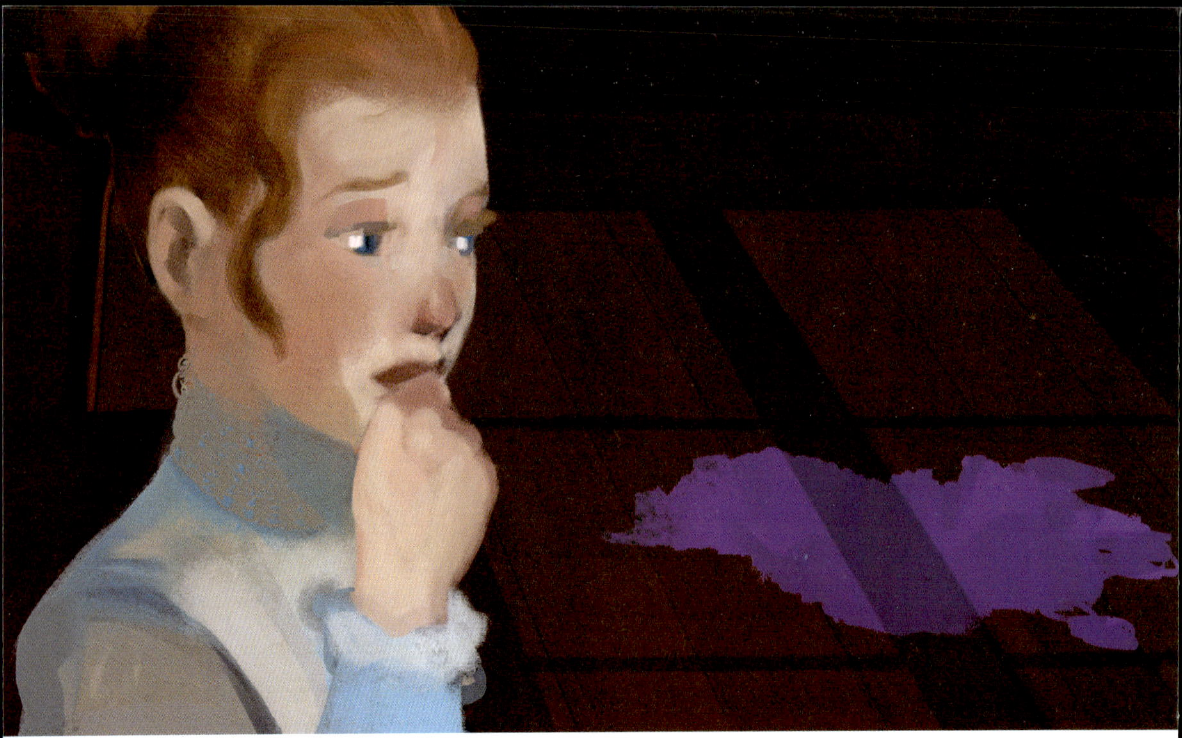

CHAPTER **FOUR**

The Ghost Laughs

track 07

The next morning at breakfast the Otis family talked about the ghost.

'We hit him with our pillows,' laughed the twins.

'That's not nice,' said Mr Otis. 'That poor ghost lived in this house for centuries. We must respect him. But if he doesn't use the "Rising Sun Lubricator", we'll take his chains away from him. It's impossible to sleep with all that noise.'

Only one strange thing happened during the week. Every evening Washington cleaned the stain on the floor of the library. Every morning the stain was there again but it changed colour. One day it was red. Then it was purple. On another day it was bright green.

Everyone in the family thought this was very funny.

'It's the funniest thing in the world!' said the twins, laughing.

Only Virginia did not laugh. She was very upset, but no one knew why.

The Ghost Laughs

On Sunday night, the ghost appeared again.

The family heard a loud noise in the hall and they ran downstairs quickly. They saw an old suit of armour on the floor and the Canterville ghost was sitting on a chair. He wanted to put on an old suit of armour and frighten the family, but it was too heavy for him. The armour fell and hurt him, and now his old bones hurt a lot. He was very unhappy and looked at the old armour that belonged to his family.

The twins were very excited when they saw this. They ran upstairs to their room and got their peashooters. Then they shot at the ghost with their peashooters and laughed.

Mr Otis went to get his gun and pointed it at the ghost. 'Hold up your hands!' said Mr Otis, looking at the ghost.

The ghost was very angry and surprised. He looked at Mr Otis and at the gun with his red eyes. Then he changed into a mist and ran away.

Washington was standing near Mr Otis and his candle suddenly went out. It was completely dark in the big hall.

'Now I'll show them my terrible laugh,' thought the ghost. 'This is the perfect time. It's my loudest laugh. Their hair will turn white when they hear it. Famous lords, ladies and servants ran out of the house when they heard this terrible laugh three hundred years ago, And they never returned!'

'Haaa! Haaa! Haaa!' The ghost's laugh was loud and terrible. It filled the house.

At that moment Mrs Otis came out of her bedroom. She was calm and had a bottle of medicine in her hand.

'Sir, I don't think you're feeling well,' she said, 'You probably have a bad stomach ache. Take this medicine, It's made in the United

States of America and it's excellent. It'll make you feel better immediately. And let me know if you want another bottle.'

The ghost looked at Mrs Otis angrily.

'What!' he thought. 'I don't want any medicine! I don't have a stomach ache. How can I frighten these Americans? Perhaps I can change into a big black dog. That will certainly frighten them.'

But just then he heard the twins. They were coming with their peashooters.

'Oh no, those terrible twins!' he thought.

The ghost immediately disappeared and went to his secret room. He was very sad.

'I failed,' he thought. 'Why aren't these Americans afraid of me? What's wrong with me? I was such an excellent ghost in the past. Everyone was afraid of me.'

He sat down and thought about all the terrible things he did for three hundred years. He was probably one of the best ghosts in all of England.

He was ill for a few days. He did not leave his room except to put back the bloodstain in the library that Washington cleaned every time. He always remembered the bloodstain because it was a very important part of his job.

'I must get better,' thought the ghost. 'Then I'll plan a *terrible* revenge for the Otis family.'

UNDERSTANDING THE TEXT

1 KEY **COMPREHENSION CHECK**

Read the paragraph below and choose the best word – A, B or C – for each space. There is an example at the beginning (0).

The Otis family talked (**0**) ....C.... the ghost at breakfast. The twins laughed (**1**) .... they hit him with (**2**) .... pillows. They did not respect him. Washington cleaned the stain (**3**) .... the floor of the library every evening. But every morning it was there (**4**) .... with a different colour.

One night the Otis family (**5**) .... a loud noise in the hall and saw a suit of armour on the floor. The ghost was (**6**) .... near it. The suit of armour was very heavy and hurt (**7**) .... when it fell. Mr Otis then pointed a gun at the ghost.

The twins laughed and Sir Simon was very angry. He showed them his terrible laugh but no one was frightened. Mrs Otis thought he was ill and gave him some medicine for his (**8**) .... Sir Simon was very sad and angry. (**9**) .... three hundred years everyone was afraid of him, but the Americans were not. He (**10**) .... to plan a terrible revenge.

0	**A** to	**B** of	**C** about
1	**A** because	**B** why	**C** so
2	**A** his	**B** their	**C** a
3	**A** on	**B** in	**C** at
4	**A** too	**B** still	**C** again
5	**A** heard	**B** saw	**C** felt
6	**A** seat	**B** sit	**C** sitting
7	**A** him	**B** he	**C** his
8	**A** stomach ache	**B** toothache	**C** headache
9	**A** At	**B** During	**C** For
10	**A** decide	**B** decided	**C** deciding

2 **SPEAKING**

What did you do yesterday? Talk with a partner and tell him/her what you did and what time you did it. You can use some of the events in the box to help you.

> wake up   get up   have a shower or bath   have breakfast
> brush teeth   get dressed   go to school   catch a bus/train
> have lunch   go home   play a sport   play a musical instrument
> do homework   have dinner   wash the dishes
> turn on your computer   watch TV   go to bed

3 THE TIME
What time is it? Write the time in numbers and in letters under each picture.

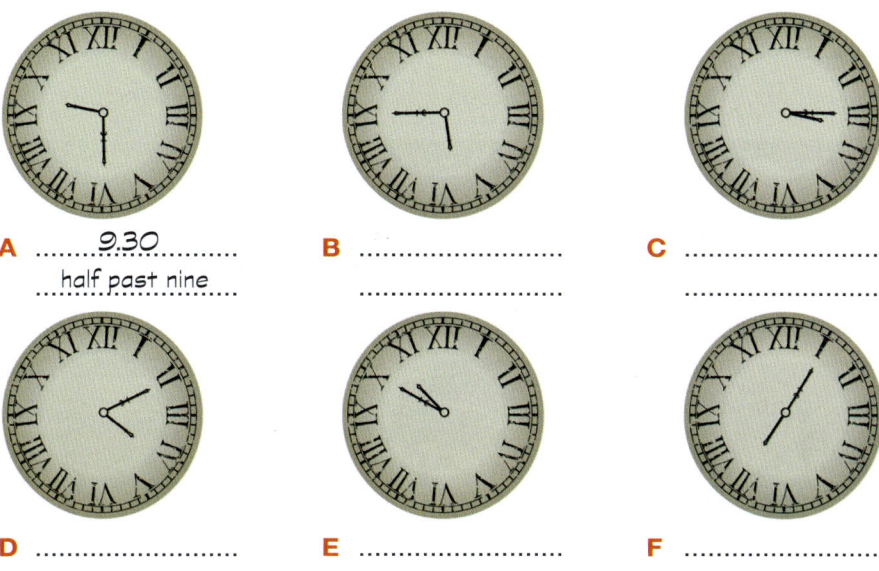

A ....9.30..........
....half past nine....

B ....
....

C ....
....

D ....
....

E ....
....

F ....
....

4 KNIGHTS AND SUITS OF ARMOUR
Complete the paragraph with the Past Simple of the verbs in the box below. Some verbs can be used more than once.

take part	go	protect	wear (x2)	ride	fight	be (x2)	come

In the Middle Ages knights (**1**) .... important soldiers. They
(**2**) .... from rich and noble families and they (**3**) .... for
their king and their country. It (**4**) .... a great honour to become a
knight. Knights (**5**) .... horses and (**6**) .... heavy suits of
armour. This armour (**7**) .... the knights during battles. Even their
horses (**8**) .... heavy armour.

Tournaments were a favourite sport in the Middle Ages. Knights
(**9**) .... in these tournaments. Many people (**10**) .... to see
their favourite knights fight in the tournaments.

5 SPEAKING
Do you know any stories about King Arthur and the Knights of the Round Table?

BEFORE YOU READ

1 **VOCABULARY**

Match the words with their meanings. Use a dictionary if necessary.

1 dagger   **3** sword   **5** pumpkin

2 skeleton   **4** furious   **6** terrified

 **A**

 **B**

 **C**

 **D**

 **E**

 **F**

2 **LISTENING**

Listen to Chapter Five and and choose the correct answer – A, B or C.

track 08

1 When did the ghost plan his revenge?

    A ☐ For Sunday, 19 August

    B ☐ For Friday, 17 August

    C ☐ For Thursday, 16 August

2 What colour was the ghost's hat?

    A ☐ White

    B ☐ Black

    C ☐ Red

3 What was the weather like that night?

    A ☐ Stormy

    B ☐ Cold

    C ☐ Foggy

4 What did the ghost have in his hand?

    A ☐ A sword

    B ☐ A dagger

    C ☐ A white bed sheet

CHAPTER FIVE

The Terrible Twins

track 08

The ghost planned his revenge for Friday, 17 August. He looked at all his old clothes carefully and decided what to wear.

'I'll wear this big red hat and this white bed sheet,' thought the ghost. 'I'll take this old dagger and go to Washington's bedroom. I hate that boy because he always removes my bloodstain. First I'll wake him up and then I'll stab [1] myself in the neck three times with the old dagger. He'll shout in terror.

'Then I'll go to his parents' room and I'll put my cold hands on Mrs Otis's face and say frightening things in Mr Otis's ears.

'Finally I'll go to the twins' room. I'll stand between their beds in the form of a dead body. I'll take off the white sheet and become a skeleton. I'll walk around their room and make all kinds of strange noises. They'll be terrified.

1. **stab** : (verb) to penetrate with a pointed weapon.

'But I don't know what to do with Miss Virginia. She never laughs at me, and she's pretty and kind. Perhaps I won't frighten her.'

There was a big storm that night. It was raining and very windy. He looked outside the window and smiled; he loved this kind of weather.

'It's the perfect night for my revenge,' he thought.

For some time he could hear the twins. They were laughing and making noise in their bedroom. But at a quarter past eleven everything was silent.

'Three hundred years ago I killed my wife,' he said. 'And now I'll do another terrible thing!'

At midnight the ghost walked quietly in the dark hall with a terrible smile on his face. He came near Washington's bedroom with the old dagger in his hand.

But as he turned the corner he stopped with a cry of terror.

'Aaaaaaaaaaaaagh!!!'

There, in front of him, was a horrible ghost.

It had a round, fat face. Fire came from its eyes and mouth, and it was wearing a long white sheet. It had a sword in his hand. There was a big notice on the sheet.

Sir Simon was terrified because he never saw a ghost before. He ran back to his secret room and sat on his bed in the dark. He was really frightened.

The next morning he decided to go and look for the other ghost. 'Perhaps two ghosts are better than one,' he thought. 'He could be my friend and we could work together to frighten the Americans, especially the twins.' But when he found the other ghost, he was very surprised. There was no fire in its eyes and its sword was on the floor.

He ran to help it, but he discovered that it was only a white sheet, a pumpkin and a kitchen knife.

The text visible within the image reads:

THE OTIS GHOST
THE ONLY TRUE AND
ORIGINAL SPIRIT...
IGNORE ALL IMITATIONS

He read the notice:

> **THE OTIS GHOST,**
> **THE ONLY TRUE AND ORIGINAL SPIRIT...**
> **IGNORE² ALL IMITATIONS!**

Suddenly he understood. This was a trick³ – the twins' terrible trick!

Simon de Canterville was furious. He raised his arms in anger and said some terrible words. He wanted revenge. But now he was very tired and went back to his room to rest.

The next day he was not feeling well. The excitement of the last four weeks made him very tired. For five days he did not even put back the bloodstain in the library.

'The Otis family comes from a modern country with no history,' he thought. 'They don't understand the job of a ghost.'

Simon de Canterville's job was to haunt Canterville Chase. Three hundred years ago he promised to do this. So every Saturday night he walked along the halls between midnight and three o'clock. He took off his shoes and walked quietly. He used 'Rising Sun Lubricator' on his chains. He didn't want to make a noise, because he was afraid of the twins.

However, the twins continued to play tricks on him. He often fell down the stairs because the twins put butter on them.

Sir Simon was really furious and thought, 'I must be clever and plan another horrible revenge – a revenge that no one will forget!'

2. **ignore** : (verb) don't look at or do not pay attention to something/someone.
3. **trick** : a bad joke.

UNDERSTANDING THE TEXT

1 **KEY** **COMPREHENSION CHECK**
Read the sentences about Chapter Five. Choose the correct answer – A, B or C. There is an example at the beginning (0).

0 The ghost decided to wear
- **A** ☐ a suit of armour.
- **B** ☐ a big red hat and a long white shirt.
- **C** ☑ a big red hat and a white bed sheet.

1 The ghost hated Washington
- **A** ☐ because he threw pillows at him.
- **B** ☐ because he laughed at him.
- **C** ☐ because he always cleaned the bloodstain.

2 The ghost wanted to put his cold hands
- **A** ☐ on Mr Otis's ears.
- **B** ☐ on Mrs Otis's face.
- **C** ☐ on the twins faces.

3 The ghost walked quietly in the dark hall
- **A** ☐ with a candle in his hand.
- **B** ☐ with a sword in his hand.
- **C** ☐ with a dagger in his hand.

4 The ghost was terrified
- **A** ☐ when he saw another ghost in the hall.
- **B** ☐ when he heard the twins laughing in their bedroom.
- **C** ☐ when he looked outside the window and saw the storm.

5 The twins made the Otis ghost
- **A** ☐ with a suit of armour and a white sheet.
- **B** ☐ with a pumpkin, a white sheet and a sword.
- **C** ☐ with a white sheet, a pumpkin and a kitchen knife.

6 Sir Simon continued to haunt Canterville Chase
- **A** ☐ but only on Sunday night.
- **B** ☐ but he didn't make any noise.
- **C** ☐ with the Otis ghost.

HE TOOK OFF HIS SHOES AND WALKED *QUIETLY.*

The word **quietly** is an adverb. We use adverbs with verbs to tell us 'how' something happens.

We form most adverbs by adding **–ly** to an adjective.

adjective	adverb
quiet	quiet**ly**
silent	silent**ly**

But when the adjective ends in a **consonant** + **y**, we change the 'y' to **-ily**.

*easy – eas**ily***   *angry – angr**ily***

When an adjective ends in **-ful** we double the 'l'.

careful – carefully   *thoughtful – thoughtfully*

Be careful! The adverbs of 'good' and 'fast' are irregular.

*good – **well***   *fast – **fast***

2 ADVERBS

Fill in the gaps with the correct form of the adverb. Use the adjectives in the box below.

good	careful	quick	easy	happy	soft	slow

1 Sir Simon choose his clothes ....

2 When Sir Simon saw the Otis ghost he ran away ....

3 Sir Simon wasn't feeling .... for a week.

4 The twins played .... in their bedroom.

5 Mrs Umney walked .... because she was old.

6 'I can clean the stain .... with 'Pinkerton's Champion Cleaner',' said Washington.

7 'Please speak .... because the children are sleeping,' said Mrs Otis.

T: GRADE 3

3 SPEAKING – FREE TIME

Virginia likes riding her pony in her free time. Use these questions to talk to the class about what you do in your free time.

1 What are three things you do in your free time?

2 How often do you do them?

3 Are they easy, difficult or dangerous to do?

4 Why do you like them?

5 Who do you do them with?

4 KEY CONVERSATION

Complete the conversation (0-5) with the phrases (A-H) below. There is an example at the beginning (0).

Washington: Do you want to go riding with me tomorrow?
Virginia: (**0**) .....E...
Washington: Are you taking your new pony?
Virginia: (**1**) ....
Washington: Where do you want to ride?
Virginia: (**2**) ....
Washington: What time do you want to leave?
Virginia: (**3**) ....
Washington: Let's bring a picnic.
Virginia: (**4**) ....
Washington: Good! I'll bring the drinks.
Virginia: (**5**) ....

A Only fruit juice, please.
B Before noon.
C Yes, I am.
D Near the lake.
E Yes, I'm free tomorrow.
F Yes, I like it.
G I'll make some sandwiches.
H It's late

5 PREPOSITIONS

Complete the sentences 1-7 with the prepositions in the box below.

inside	with	under	on	for	in	at

1 There was a big stain .... the floor.
2 The twins played ball .... the garden.
3 Pinkerton's Champion Cleaner was .... Washington's suitcase.
4 The Otis family had dinner .... seven o'clock.
5 'This letter is .... you, Mr Otis,' said Mrs Umney.
6 'Do you want to go to London .... me?' asked Mrs Otis.
7 Virginia was sitting on the grass .... a big tree.

BEFORE YOU READ

1 **VOCABULARY**

Match the words with their meaning. Use a dictionary if necessary.

1 Headless   **2** Jug   **3** Chimney   **4** Vampire

 A

 B

 C

 D

2 **LISTENING**

track 09

Listen to Chapter Six and and choose the correct answer – A, B or C.

1 When did Sir Simon appear as 'the Headless Lord'?

   A ☐ Seventy years ago.

   B ☐ Seventeen years ago.

   C ☐ Sixty years ago.

2 Why did Sir Simon run back to his room?

   A ☐ Because he forgot his chains.

   B ☐ Because he was wet and cold.

   C ☐ Because he was sleepy.

3 What did Sir Simon see downstairs in the hall?

   A ☐ An old painting of the Canterville family.

   B ☐ Large photographs of Mr and Mrs Otis.

   C ☐ A jug of water.

4 Who gave a wonderful party in the gardens of Canterville Chase?

   A ☐ Virginia and Cecil.

   B ☐ Mr Otis.

   C ☐ Mrs Otis.

3 **READING PICTURES**

Look at the picture on page 49 and answer the question.

What are the people at the garden party doing?

CHAPTER SIX

A Horrible Revenge

'This time I'll appear as the Headless Lord,' thought the ghost. 'I'll frighten them all. Seventy years ago I appeared as the Headless Lord in front of young Lady Barbara. She immediately ran away and never returned to Canterville Chase. It was a great success!'

He took three hours to get ready, since he had to choose the right clothes carefully. Then in the middle of the night he walked silently to the twins' bedroom. He pushed the door open and... a big, heavy jug of water fell on him. He was completely wet. The twins sat up in their beds and laughed loudly. They couldn't stop laughing.

The poor ghost ran back to his secret room. He was wet and cold. The next day he wasn't feeling well because he had a very bad cold.

'I can't frighten this American family,' he thought sadly. 'I tried everything, but I failed. However, I must continue to haunt Canterville Chase; it's my job and now I'll do it quietly.'

One night he was downstairs in the hall. He saw large photographs of Mr and Mrs Otis.

'Where are the old paintings of the Canterville family?' he thought. 'These Americans know nothing about our long history.'

He wanted to go to the library to see if the bloodstain was still there, but suddenly two dark figures jumped out of a corner.

'BOO!!!' they shouted loudly in his ear.

The ghost was terribly frightened and jumped into the fireplace and climbed up the chimney to his room. After this horrible adventure nobody saw him at night.

The Otis family began to live a normal life and didn't think about the ghost any more. Mr Otis wrote a history of the American Government. Mrs Otis gave a wonderful party in the beautiful gardens of Canterville Chase. There was a lot of good American food and people played American games.

Cecil, the young Duke of Cheshire, came to stay at Canterville Chase. Virginia rode her pony in the country with Cecil. He was in love with Virginia.

Mr Otis wrote to Lord Canterville: 'The ghost went away.'

'Congratulations to you and your wife,' answered the Lord.

Everything seemed perfect at Canterville Chase. But Mr Otis was very wrong. The ghost was still in his secret room, but he was tired and ill. He knew that Cecil was in the house.

'I frightened his grandfather, the old Duke of Cheshire, a hundred years ago,' he thought. 'Tonight I'll dress like a horrible vampire and frighten the young Duke, Cecil. I'll show him that I'm still terrifying.'

The ghost got ready to haunt the house again, but at the last moment he remembered the terrible twins. So he decided to stay in his room forever. That night Cecil slept well in his warm bed and dreamt about Virginia.

UNDERSTANDING THE TEXT

1 **COMPREHENSION CHECK**

Are these sentences 'Right' (A) or 'Wrong' (B)? If there is not enough information to answer 'Right' (A) or 'Wrong' (B), choose 'Doesn't say' (C). There is an example at the beginning (0).

		A	B	C
0	Sir Simon was a friend of the Headless Lord.	☐	✓	☐
1	Lady Barbara was not afraid of the Headless Lord.	☐	☐	☐
2	Sir Simon spent three hours getting ready.	☐	☐	☐
3	The twins laughed loudly because Sir Simon got completely wet.	☐	☐	☐
4	The ghost took the jug and threw it on the floor angrily.	☐	☐	☐
5	The ghost saw three big photographs of Mr and Mrs Otis in the hall.	☐	☐	☐
6	The twins shouted 'Boo!' in the ghost's ear while he was sitting in his secret room.	☐	☐	☐
7	Mr Otis wrote to Lord Canterville and told him that the ghost went away.	☐	☐	☐
8	Mrs Otis wrote a book about the history of English ghosts.	☐	☐	☐
9	Cecil, the young Duke of Cheshire, came to visit the Otis family for a week.	☐	☐	☐
10	Cecil, the young Duke of Cheshire, was twenty years old.	☐	☐	☐
11	Sir Simon wanted to appear as the Headless Lord and frighten Cecil.	☐	☐	☐
12	Sir Simon decided to leave Canterville Chase because he was afraid of the twins.	☐	☐	☐

T: GRADE 4

2 **FOOD**

There was a lot of good American food at Mrs Otis's party.
Talk about food with your partner. Use these questions to help you.

1 What is your favourite food?
2 Where do you eat it?
3 What food do you hate.
4 Who cooks at your house?
5 Do you like food from other countries?

3 WRITING

Virginia received a postcard from Dorothy, her best friend in Boston. She wants to write her a postcard from London. Answer Dorothy's questions and write between 25-35 words.

Dear Virginia,
It's summer here in Boston and the weather is hot. I go swimming at the beach almost every day. It's great fun!
What's England like? Do you like it? What do you do every day? Do you have any new friends? Please send me a postcard.
Love, Dorothy

Dear Dorothy,
Thank you for the nice postcard...

....

....

....

....

....

....

4 QUESTION WORDS

Fill in the gaps with the correct question word: *when*, *how*, *who*, *where*, *what*, *why*. Then find the answer below.

1   .... did Mr Otis see outside his bedroom? .....
2   .... did the Otis family get to Canterville Chase? .....
3   .... did Sir Simon get angry? .....
4   .... did Mrs Umney faint? .....
5   .... did the Otis family come from? .....
6   .... did Mrs Otis give Sir Simon? .....

A   Because the Otis family had no respect for him.
B   She gave him a bottle of medicine.
C   They took a carriage from the train station.
D   She fainted when she heard the thunder and lightning.
E   He saw the ghost of Sir Simon.
F   They came from the United States of America.

5 **KEY** LISTENING

track 10

The Otis family take a tour of London during the late 1890s. Listen to what the guide tells them and choose the correct answer – A, B or C.

1 How many parks are there in London?

A ☐   B ☐   C ☐

2 What can you do on The Serpentine Lake?

A ☐   B ☐   C ☐

3 Where is Big Ben?

A ☐   B ☐   C ☐

4 When was Tower Bridge completed?

A ☐   B ☐   C ☐

5 What can you see at the Tower of London?

A ☐   B ☐   C ☐

BEFORE YOU READ

1 VOCABULARY

Match the words with their meaning. Use a dictionary if necessary.

1	☐ tore	A	Famous English school for children of rich families.
2	☐ mend	B	(verb: to tear—tore, torn) made a hole in.
3	☐ ugly	C	Make someone angry.
4	☐ Eton	D	To repair.
5	☐ disturb	E	Not polite.
6	☐ rude	F	Opposite of beautiful.

2 LISTENING

Track 11

Listen to Chapter Seven and choose the right answer – A, B or C.

1 Where did Virginia and Cecil go?
A ☐ They went riding.
B ☐ They went to the theatre.
C ☐ They went to the park.

2 Who did Virginia see in one of the rooms of Canterville Chase?
A ☐ Her mother's servant.
B ☐ Her mother.
C ☐ The ghost of Sir Simon.

3 Why must Sir Simon make noise with his chains and frighten people?
A ☐ Because he is bad.
B ☐ Because he has nothing else to do.
C ☐ Because it is a ghost's job.

4 How did Sir Simon die?
A ☐ He died because he did not have any food or water.
B ☐ He died because his wife's brothers killed him with a sword.
C ☐ He died because he fell down the stairs.

5 What did Sir Simon steal?
A ☐ 'Pinkerton's Champion Cleaner'.
B ☐ Virginia's paints.
C ☐ A sandwich.

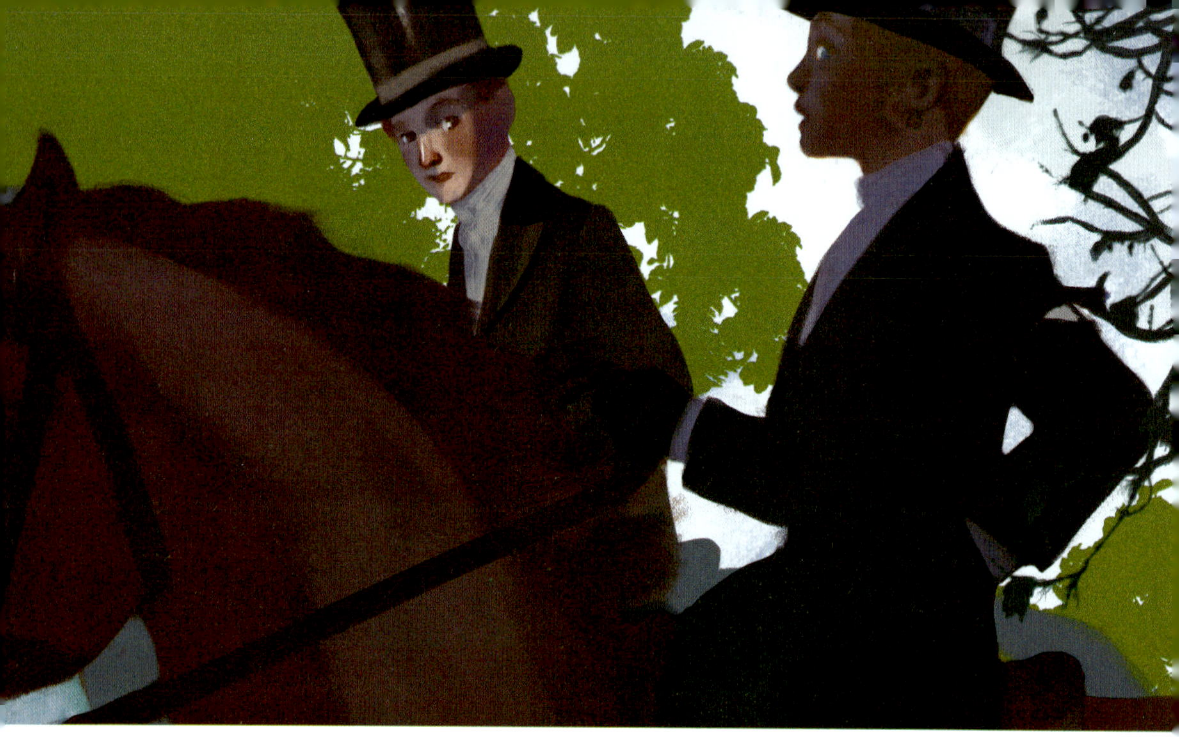

CHAPTER **SEVEN**

Virginia and Sir Simon

track 11

The next day Virginia and Cecil went riding together on their ponies. Virginia rode too close to a tree and tore her jacket. When they returned to Canterville Chase, Virginia wanted to mend her jacket. But she didn't want anyone to see her torn jacket so she went up the back stairs. The door of one of the rooms was open and there was someone inside.

'Perhaps it's my mother's servant and she can mend my jacket,' she thought.

She went inside the room quietly. She was very surprised when she saw the Canterville Ghost, who was sitting by the window. He was looking sadly at the red and yellow autumn leaves outside the window. At first Virginia wanted to run away to her room. But the poor ghost looked very unhappy and Virginia felt sorry for him. She decided to speak to him.

'I am very sorry for you,' said Virginia softly. 'My twin brothers are

Virginia and Sir Simon

going away to Eton tomorrow. After that, if you're good no one will disturb you.'

Sir Simon was surprised and he looked at the pretty girl.

'Don't ask me to be good,' he said. 'I'm a ghost. I must make a noise with my chains. I must frighten people. I must walk about at night. It's my job.'

'I know you were bad in the past,' said Virginia. 'Mrs Umney told us that you killed your wife.'

'Yes, that's true,' said the ghost.

'It's wrong to kill someone,' said Virginia.

The ghost was angry and said, 'My wife was ugly and she cooked badly. She never looked after my clothes. And after she died her brothers took revenge. They put me in a room without any food or water until I died. That wasn't very nice of them!'

'Oh, Mr Ghost – I mean Sir Simon – are you hungry? I have a sandwich here. Do you want it?'

'No, thank you,' said the ghost. 'Ghosts don't eat anything. But it's very kind of you. You're much nicer than your horrible, rude, dishonest family.'

'Stop!' cried Virginia. 'You're rude and dishonest! You stole my paints and used them to put the bloodstain on the floor of the library. That's why it was sometimes red, sometimes purple, sometimes green. I couldn't paint any more because you took my colours.'

'Yes,' said the ghost, 'but it's very difficult to get real blood these days. Your horrible brother cleaned the stain every day with his "Pinkerton's Champion Cleaner". I had to use your paints. You Americans don't understand ghosts.'

Now Virginia was angry too.

'You know nothing about my country. You must come to America

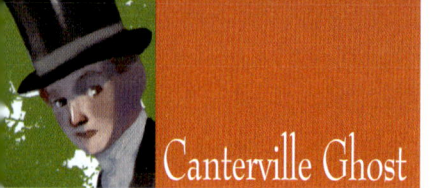

and then you'll understand many things. My father will get you a free ticket. You'll be a great success in New York.

'New York!' said the ghost, who was surprised.

'Yes, New York,' said Virginia.

'What's it like?' asked the ghost.

'It's America's biggest and most important city,' said Virginia. 'It's on the Atlantic coast and there are a lot of big buildings, shops, theatres, parks and other interesting things.'

'Oh, really,' said the ghost, looking at Virginia.

'You know, a lot of Americans haven't got, a grandfather and they'll pay a hundred thousand dollars to have one,' said Virginia. 'And they'll pay much more for a family ghost.'

'I don't think I'll like America,' said the ghost. 'You have no history. All you have is money and bad manners.' [1]

'Goodbye,' said Virginia angrily. 'You're very rude. I'll go and get the twins.'

'Oh, please don't go, Miss Virginia,' cried the ghost. 'I'm very lonely and unhappy. I don't know what to do. I want to sleep but I can't.'

'That's impossible,' said Virginia. 'Just go to bed and close your eyes. It's not difficult to sleep. Even little babies know how to sleep.'

'The last time I slept was three hundred years ago,' said the ghost sadly. 'I'm so *tired*.'

'Three hundred years ago!' said Virginia, looking at the tired face of the old ghost. 'That's really a very long time.'

1. **bad manners** : behaviour that isn't polite.

UNDERSTANDING THE TEXT

1 KEY COMPREHENSION CHECK

Read the paragraph below and choose the correct word for each space – A, B or C. There is an example at the beginning.

Virginia and Cecil went (0) ...B... together and Virginia (1) .... her jacket. When she returned to Canterville Chase she looked (2) .... someone to (3) .... it. In one of the rooms of Canterville Chase she saw Sir Simon, the Canterville ghost. He was looking outside the window and he was (4) .... sad. Virginia decided to talk to him and said, 'My twin brothers are going to Eton tomorrow. After that if you are good no one will disturb you.'

The ghost (5) .... Virginia that he had to make noise and frighten people. It was (6) .... job. In the past he killed his wife (7) .... she was a bad cook and never looked after his clothes. His wife's brothers took revenge. They put Sir Simon in a room without (8) .... food or water until he died.

Virginia got angry because the ghost (9) .... her paints. He used them to put the bloodstain (10) .... the floor of the library. Now he was very tired because the last time he slept was three hundred years ago.

0	A	driving	B	riding	C	walking
1	A	tore	B	cut	C	broke
2	A	after	B	for	C	at
3	A	do	B	repair	C	mend
4	A	very	B	much	C	many
5	A	spoke	B	told	C	said
6	A	his	B	its	C	him
7	A	after	B	because	C	why
8	A	any	B	no	C	some
9	A	stealing	B	steal	C	stole
10	A	under	B	on	C	in

T: GRADE 3

2 SPEAKING - PLACES IN THE LOCAL AREA

Canterville Chase is near the lovely town of Ascot, in eastern England. It is an interesting place to visit. Think about your local area and tell the class about two places of interest. Use these questions to help you.

1 Why are these places interesting?
2 How often do you visit them?
3 What do you do when you're there?
4 How do you get there: by car, bus, boat or on foot?

3 KEY NOTICES

Which notice (A-H) says this (1-5)? There is an example at the beginning (0).

0   ..D.. An important battle took place here.
1   ..... Things here are cheaper this week.
2   ..... People here are friendly.
3   ..... On Sundays you can't take the train for London from platform one.
4   ..... You can't buy a pet bird here.
5   ..... You mustn't eat here.

A

ASCOT TRAIN STATION

Trains for London leave from platform 1

On weekends please use platform 3

B

SIR HENRY'S BOOKSHOP

Since 1789 - Books and dictionaries in all languages

Special prices this week only!

C

ASCOT PUBLIC LIBRARY

Open all year - 9 am to 7 pm

No food allowed inside

D

BRITISH HISTORICAL SITE

Battle of Hastings - 1066

Guides available on weekends

E

LONDON CITY HOSPITAL

Please use main entrance

Leave horses and carriages at the back entrance

Silence at all hours!

F

PENELOPE'S PET SHOP

Dogs and cats for sale

Open mornings only

G

Dr James Bentley, Dentist

By appointment only.

Monday, Wednesday and Friday

H

SALLY'S BAKERY

Open 8 am to 6 pm

Service with smile!

BEFORE YOU READ

1 **READING PICTURES**
Look at the picture on page 63 and answer the questions.

1 Where do you think Virginia and Sir Simon are doing?
2 What can they see in front of them?
3 How do you think Virginia feels?

2 **LISTENING**
Listen to Chapter Eight and choose the correct answer – A, B or C.

track 12

1 Virginia looked at the ghost
   A ☐ and was frightened.
   B ☐ and was very surprised.
   C ☐ and started crying.

2 Sir Simon wanted to go to
   A ☐ the woods.
   B ☐ Ascot.
   C ☐ the Garden of Sleep.

3 The old writing on the library window
   A ☐ had six lines.
   B ☐ had two lines.
   C ☐ had ten lines.

4 Virginia did not go downstairs
   A ☐ for dinner.
   B ☐ for breakfast.
   C ☐ for tea.

5 Mrs Otis was worried because Virginia did not appear
   A ☐ at six o'clock.
   B ☐ at half past six.
   C ☐ at quarter past six.

6 The Duke of Cheshire could not go and look for Virginia
   A ☐ because he didn't have a horse.
   B ☐ because he was too young.
   C ☐ because he was not feeling well.

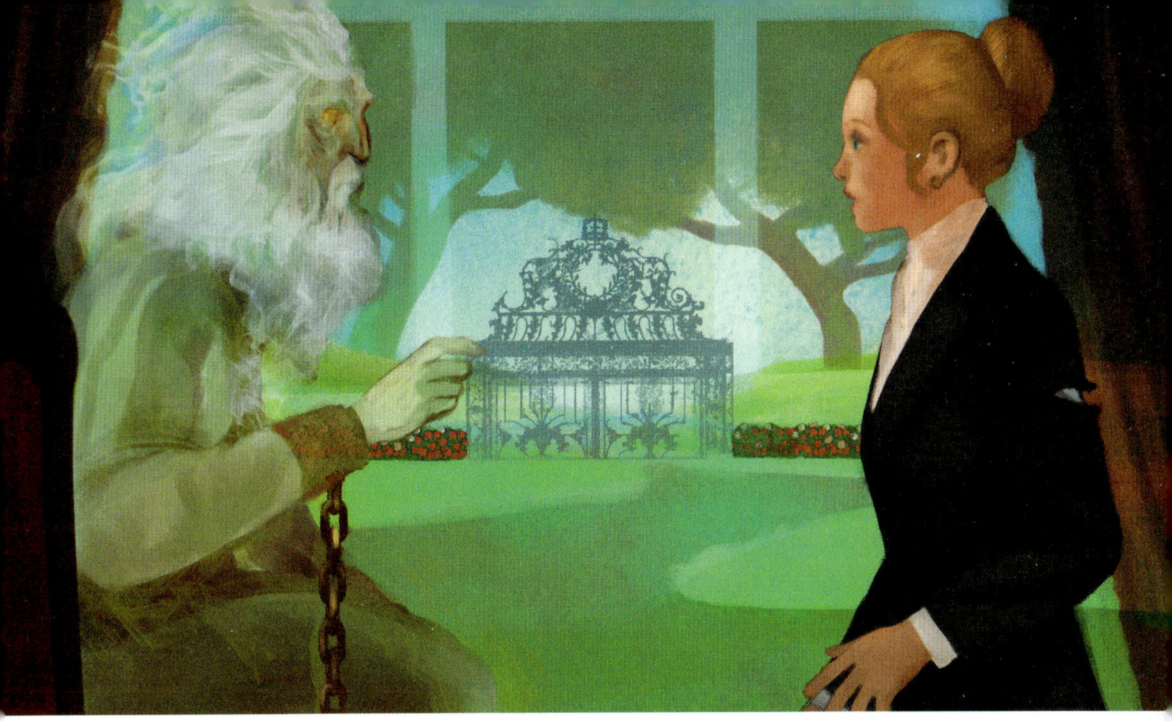

CHAPTER **EIGHT**

The Garden of Sleep

Virginia looked at the ghost with her beautiful blue eyes and was very surprised. She went to his side and looked up at his tired old face. track 12

'Poor, poor ghost,' she said softly. 'Isn't there a place where you can sleep?'

'Far away, on the other side of the woods,' he said in a low voice, 'there's a little garden. The grass is green and soft. There are big old trees and white flowers. And little birds sing all the time.'

'You mean the Garden of Sleep,' said Virginia.

'Yes, the Garden of Sleep,' said the ghost. 'Sleep is so beautiful. I want to lie in that silent garden and forget everything. There I can finally sleep.'

He looked into Virginia's blue eyes.

'You can help me, Virginia. You can open the gates [1] of the garden for me, because you have Love. Love is stronger than anything.'

1. **gates** :

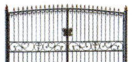

Virginia was afraid. She suddenly felt very cold. For a few moments there was silence.

Then the ghost spoke again. 'Did you see the old writing on the library window?'

'Yes, I saw it many times,' said Virginia. 'I know it well. There are six lines. They say that a young girl with blonde hair will help a bad man to pray.[2] The black trees will have flowers. A child will cry...'

'Then the house will be quiet and calm. And peace will come to Canterville,' said the ghost.

'But what does it mean?' asked Virginia.

'It means,' he said sadly, 'that you must cry for me because I can't cry. You must pray for me because I have no words. If you're good and kind, the Angel of Sleep will forgive[3] me. You'll see terrible things that will frighten you. Bad voices will speak to you. But no one will hurt you because you are so good.'

Virginia was silent for a few moments. The ghost was very sad and looked down at her blonde hair. Suddenly she stood up with a strange light in her eyes. 'I'm not afraid,' she said. 'Take me to the Garden of Sleep. I will ask the Angel of Sleep to forgive you.'

The ghost stood up with a cry of happiness. He took Virginia's hand and kissed it. His fingers were cold like ice and his lips were hot like fire.

Virginia followed the ghost across the dark room. She heard voices that said, 'Go back! Go back, little Virginia!' The ghost held her hand and she closed her eyes. Horrible animals looked at her and said, 'Be careful, Virginia! We'll never see you again if you go with him.'

---

2. **pray** : speak to God and ask for help.
3. **forgive** : when you forgive you are no longer angry with someone who did something bad to you.

The ghost walked more quickly. Virginia did not listen to the voices.

At the end of the room he stopped and said some strange words. The wall opened and in front of them it was completely black. There was a cold wind and someone pulled at her dress.

'Quickly, quickly,' cried the ghost, 'or it will be too late.'

In a moment the wall closed behind them. The room was empty.

About ten minutes later it was time for tea, but Virginia did not come downstairs. Mrs Otis sent a servant to call her. The servant returned and said, 'I can't find Miss Virginia anywhere.'

'Perhaps she went to pick flowers,' said Mrs Otis. 'She often picks flowers before dinner for the dinner table.'

At six o'clock Virginia still did not appear. Mrs Otis was worried. She sent the twins and Washington to look for her in the garden. She and Mr Otis looked for her in every room of the house. But no one was able to find her.

'Washington, let's go and look for Virginia in the park,' said Mr Otis, who was worried.

'Please let me go with you,' said the young Duke of Cheshire.

'No, Cecil you're too young,' said Mr Otis. 'Stay in the house with my wife and the twins.'

UNDERSTANDING THE TEXT

1 KEY **COMPREHENSION CHECK**

**Read the sentences about Chapter Eight. Choose the correct answer –
A, B or C. There is an example at the beginning.**

0 What is the ghost's face like?

A ☐ Terrible and frightening.

B ☑ Old and tired.

C ☐ Old and happy.

1 Where is the Garden of Sleep?

A ☐ In the woods.

B ☐ On the other side of the woods.

C ☐ Behind Canterville Chase.

2 Virginia can open the gates of the Garden of Sleep

A ☐ because she is young.

B ☐ because she never laughed at the ghost.

C ☐ because she has Love.

3 Where is the old writing?

A ☐ In an old book in the library.

B ☐ On the library window.

C ☐ On the gate of the Garden of Sleep.

4 What will Virginia ask the Angel of Sleep?

A ☐ To forgive Sir Simon.

B ☐ To pray for Sir Simon.

C ☐ To cry for Sir Simon.

5 What did Virginia do when she heard the bad voices?

A ☐ She started crying.

B ☐ She left the room and ran away.

C ☐ She didn't listen to them.

6 What did Virginia often do before dinner?

A ☐ She often picked flowers.

B ☐ She often rode her pony in the woods.

C ☐ She often read books in the library.

7 Who went to look for Virginia in the park?

A ☐ Cecil, the young Duke of Cheshire.

B ☐ Washington and Mr Otis.

C ☐ Mr and Mrs Otis.

2 KEY VOCABULARY

Read the description and write the correct word. The first letter of the word is already there.

1 Not polite. R _ _ _

2 Something you do to hurt or harm someone who has hurt or harmed you. R _ _ _ _ _ _

3 A person who looks after the house. H _ _ _ _ _ _ _ _ _ _

4 A bad joke that makes you angry. T _ _ _ _

5 Small drops of water in the air. M _ _ _

6 A copy of an original. I _ _ _ _ _ _ _ _

7 A loud noise in the sky when there is a storm. T _ _ _ _ _ _

3 OPPOSITES

Match the word (1-10) with its opposite (A-J).

1	☐ Old		A	Excited
2	☐ Silent		B	Sadness
3	☐ Love		C	Early
4	☐ Calm		D	Noisy
5	☐ Happiness		E	Dry
6	☐ Dark		F	Hot
7	☐ Late		G	Full
8	☐ Empty		H	Young
9	☐ Cold		I	Light
10	☐ Wet		J	Hate
11	☐ Ugly		K	Small
12	☐ Large		L	Beautiful

4 SPEAKING

1 What do you think will happen to Virginia?

2 Who will she see?

3 Will the Angel of Sleep forgive Sir Simon. Why or why not?

BEFORE YOU READ

1 VOCABULARY
Match the words with the pictures. Use a dictionary if necessary.

1 ☐ telegram   4 ☐ tomb
2 ☐ station master   5 ☐ jewels
3 ☐ prison cell   6 ☐ wedding

A

B

C

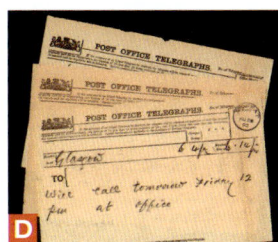
D

E

F

2 LISTENING

ck 13

Listen to the beginning of Chapter Nine and say if these sentences are true (T) or false (F).

T F

1 Mr Otis and Washington looked for Virginia everywhere. ☐☐
2 Cecil followed Mr Otis on his pony. ☐☐
3 Virginia returned in the morning. ☐☐
4 The ghost gave Virginia a box of jewels. ☐☐
5 In the small dark room Virginia and the others saw Sir Simon de Canterville's skeleton. ☐☐

3 READING PICTURES
Look at the picture on page 71 and answer the questions.

1 Describe Virginia's wedding dress and jewels.
2 How do you think Virginia and Cecil feel and why?

Looking for Virginia

Mr Otis and Washington did not find Virginia in the park. Mr Otis sent telegrams to the police. He asked them to look for a young girl. Then he rode to the nearest town and continued to look for Virginia.

The young Duke followed him on his pony. 'I'm sorry, Mr Otis. Please, don't be angry, but I'm very worried about Virginia. I must go with you. Don't send me back!'

Mr Otis looked at the young Duke and smiled kindly. 'Well, come with me then.'

They first went to the railway station. Mr Otis talked to the station master. 'Did you see my daughter?' he asked.

'No,' said the station master.

When the police arrived they looked everywhere – in every corner of Canterville Chase and in the lake. Mrs Otis was very worried.

---

1. **Scotland Yard** : central police office in London.

Looking for Virginia

'I'll telephone Scotland Yard [1] tomorrow morning,' said Mr Otis. 'They must send me some detectives immediately.'

Everyone at Canterville Chase was very sad and no one wanted to have dinner.

Mr Otis said, 'We must have something to eat.' Everyone sat down at the dinner table but no one spoke. Even the twins were quiet.

Late that night everyone was going to bed. It was midnight and suddenly there was loud thunder. There was strange music in the air. A part of the wall opened with a loud noise and Virginia appeared. She walked down the stairs. Her face was white and she had a small box in her hands.

'Virginia!' everyone cried, running to her. Mrs Otis put her arms around her. The young Duke kissed her. The twins danced a wild dance.

'What happened to you, Virginia?' asked Mr Otis, a little angrily.

'My dear Virginia,' said Mrs Otis, looking at her daughter, 'I'm so happy we found you!'

'Oh, mother,' said Virginia, 'I was with the ghost. He's dead. You must come and see him. Long ago he was very bad, but he was really sorry. He gave me this box of jewels before he died.'

The family looked at her in surprise and said, 'What do you mean?'

'Come with me and I'll show you,' said Virginia.

She took them through the opening in the wall and down a secret hall. They stopped in front of a heavy door. Virginia opened the heavy door and Washington held up his candle. They saw a small, dark room with a very small window. It was like a prison cell. A skeleton was on the floor. It was chained to a metal ring on the wall. Its right hand was near a dish and its left hand was near a jug of water on the floor. Virginia stood near the skeleton and began to pray.

'It must be the skeleton of Sir Simon de Canterville,' said Mrs Otis softly.

'Hey!' cried one of the twins. 'Look out of the window! The old black tree has flowers on it now. I can see them in the light of the moon!'

'God forgave him,' said Virginia. There was a beautiful light around her face.

'You're an angel, Virginia,' said the young Duke, and he kissed her.

Four days later there was a funeral [2] at Canterville Chase.

It started at eleven o'clock at night. Eight black horses pulled a carriage and servants walked by its side.

Lord Canterville was there and he sat with Virginia in the first carriage. Her parents were in the next carriage. Then there was Washington, the twins and the young Duke. Mrs Umney was in the last carriage.

They put the coffin with the skeleton of Sir Simon de Canterville in the ground of the old churchyard.

Virginia put some white and pink flowers on it.

The moon came out from the clouds and a bird began to sing. Virginia remembered the ghost's story of the Garden of Sleep.

She cried silently and did not say a word.

The next morning Lord Canterville said goodbye to the Otis family.

'Lord Canterville,' said Mr Otis, 'you must take the jewels that the ghost gave my daughter. They're very beautiful and very expensive. They're your family's jewels.'

'No,' said Lord Canterville, 'Virginia helped Sir Simon and the jewels belong to her. She must keep them.'

'But my daughter is only a child,' said Mr Otis. 'She doesn't need those jewels. We Americans are very simple people. We're not interested in family jewels.'

'No, Mr Otis,' said Lord Canterville, 'the jewels are hers. If I take

---

2. **funeral** : ceremony for a person who died.

them from her, Sir Simon will never forgive me. He'll come back and haunt me. Please, let Virginia keep them.'

Some time later Virginia married Cecil, the young Duke of Cheshire.

At her wedding she wore the Canterville jewels. Everyone at the wedding looked at the beautiful jewels.

Several weeks after the wedding, Virginia and Cecil visited Canterville Chase.

They walked together through the wood to Sir Simon's tomb. Virginia put some roses there. Then she sat silently and Cecil sat next to her.

'Virginia,' said the Duke, 'a wife mustn't have any secrets from her husband.'

'Dear Cecil,' said Virginia, 'I don't have any secrets.'

'Yes, you do,' said Cecil. 'You didn't tell me about you and the ghost. What happened? Where did you go with him?'

'Please don't ask me,' said Virginia. 'I can't tell you. Poor Sir Simon showed me what Life is, and how Love is stronger than anything.'

The Duke kissed her.

'You can have your secret,' he said, 'if I can have your heart.'

'You already have my heart, Cecil.'

'You'll tell your secret to our children one day, won't you?'

'Children?' Virginia said and her face became red.

UNDERSTANDING THE TEXT

1 COMPREHENSION CHECK

Are these sentences 'Right' (A) or 'Wrong' (B)? If there is not enough information to answer 'Right' (A) or 'Wrong' (B), choose 'Doesn't say' (C). There is an example at the beginning (0).

		A	B	C
0	The police looked for Virginia at the railway station.		✓	
1	Mr Otis decided to send a telegram to Scotland Yard.			
2	Washington, the twins, Cecil and Mr and Mrs Otis sat down at the dinner table at half past six, but no one was hungry.			
3	At midnight there was a loud crash of thunder and Virginia appeared on the stairs.			
4	She had a small box of jewels in her hand.			
5	Only Sir Simon's old clothes were in the small dark room.			
6	Flowers grew on the old black tree.			
7	Twenty-five people attended Sir Simon's funeral.			
8	Mr Otis did not want the Canterville family jewels.			
9	Lord Canterville sold the family jewels to Virginia.			
10	Some time after the wedding Virginia and Cecil brought flowers to Sir Simon's tomb.			
11	Virginia had a secret that she could not tell Cecil.			

2 CLASS DISCUSSION

What do you think happened to Virginia when she went with Sir Simon? Work with a partner and answer this question. Then tell your answer to the class. How many different opinions are there?

3 SPEAKING

Complete the five conversations with the correct answer – A, B or C. This is an example at the beginning (0).

0 Pass me the butter.
   A ☐ Thank you.   B ✓ Here you are. C ☐ You're welcome.

1 Are you ready?
   A ☐ Almost.   B ☐ Quite.   C ☐ Already.

2 I'll meet you at the station.
   A ☐ Please be on time. B ☐ Yes, I can.   C ☐ Yes, I do.

3 What time does the bakery open?
   A ☐ It's late.   B ☐ Not now.   C ☐ I don't know.

4 Can you come riding with me?
   A ☐ No, I'm not.   B ☐ No, I can't. C ☐ No, I don't.

4 CROSSWORD PUZZLE

Across

2

4 A person who looks after the house.

5 An expensive school for rich children.

7

8 Lovely town near Canterville Chase.

10

13 To repair, to fix.

14

Down

1

3

6 Mrs Otis comes from this city.

9

11 Not polite.

12 A copy of the original.

Oscar Wilde in the United States of America

track 14

Oscar Wilde arrived in New York City at the beginning of 1882. He planned a long tour of many important American cities where he gave lectures. [1]

Oscar Wilde began his tour in New York City and then went to Boston. Here he talked to students at Harvard University. He visited Philadelphia and met Walt Whitman and Harriet Beecher Stowe, who were two famous American writers. They enjoyed talking to Wilde.

Then he travelled to the capital of the United States, Washington D.C. and met another famous American writer, Henry James.

His lecture tour continued to the Great Lakes, Niagara Falls, Chicago and the Midwest. He crossed the American continent and even visited a silver mine [2] in Nevada.

Wilde particularly liked California because it is such a beautiful state. He also travelled to Texas and other southern states.

1. **lectures** : he talked to audiences about his writing and his ideas about art.
2. **silver mine** : a place where you can find a precious metal called silver.

Newspaper reporters followed Oscar Wilde everywhere and wrote about his lectures. Most Americans were very surprised when they saw him and listened to him. They wanted to see him because he was famous for his unusual clothes and unusual ideas about art and life. There were always a lot of people at his lectures. He was very popular at first. People invited him to dinners and he met important American people. But not everyone liked him. Many Americans thought his clothes were silly[3] and his ideas were dangerous.

During the nineteenth century many English people thought that America had a lot of money but no history or culture.[4] Wilde used these ideas as a source of humour. In *The Canterville Ghost* Oscar Wilde shows that Americans have many good qualities.

Wilde gave 140 lectures in different cities in 260 days! He made a lot of money on his American tour. At the end of his tour he said, 'America is not a country – it is a world.'

1 COMPREHENSION CHECK
Circle the correct word to complete the sentence.

1 Oscar Wilde arrived in the United States at the *end / beginning* of 1882.
2 Wilde met Walt Whitman and Harriet Beecher Stowe in *Philadelphia / Washington D.C.*
3 Wilde visited a silver mine in *Texas / Nevada*.
4 *University students / Newspaper reporters* followed Wilde everywhere during his tour.
5 *Everyone / Not everyone* liked Oscar Wilde.
6 Many Americans thought his clothes were *ugly / silly*.

2 DISCUSSION
1 What do you think Oscar Wilde meant when he said, 'America is not a country—it is a world.' ?
2 Name three things that you know about America.

---

3. **silly** : foolish, ridiculous, not serious.
4. **culture** : knowledge of the arts — music, painting, literature.

Filmography

Title:	The Canterville Ghost
Date:	1944
Director:	Jules Dassin
Actors:	Charles Laughton, Robert Young

 Look at the stills [1] and answer the questions.

1 How old is Virginia in this still?
2 Where is she and what is she doing?
3 Describe the ghost.
4 What page of the story does this still refer to?
5 Write you own caption [2] for this still.

Title:	The Canterville Ghost
Date:	1966
Director:	Syd Macartney
Actors:	Patrick Stewart, Neve Campbell

1 Who are the two characters?
2 How is Virginia different from the first still?
3 How is the ghost different from the first still?
4 Write your own caption for this still.

1. **still** : (here) a photograph of the scene of a film.
2. **caption** : words printed near a picture that explain something about the picture.

AFTER READING

1 COMPREHENSION CHECK

Are the following sentences true (T) or false (F)? Correct the false ones.

T F

1. The Otis family came from the United States and did not want to live in a haunted house. ☐ ☐
2. Lady Eleanore was the old housekeeper at Canterville Chase. ☐ ☐
3. Mrs Lucretia Otis fainted when she saw the bloodstain on the floor. ☐ ☐
4. It was easy for Washington to clean the bloodstain. ☐ ☐
5. Sir Simon killed his brother in the library in 1575. ☐ ☐
6. The ghost's chains made a lot of noise when the Otis family was sleeping. ☐ ☐
7. The ghost lived in a secret room of Canterville Chase. ☐ ☐
8. The ghost was very angry because the American family did not give him anything to eat or drink. ☐ ☐
9. The twins were always naughty and Sir Simon was afraid of them. ☐ ☐
10. The Otis ghost was not a ghost at all. ☐ ☐
11. Virginia tore her jacket while she was riding with Cecil. ☐ ☐
12. When Virginia saw Sir Simon she felt sorry for him. ☐ ☐
13. Virginia went with Sir Simon and asked the Angel of Sleep to forgive him. ☐ ☐
14. The Otis family found Sir Simon's skeleton in the library near the bloodstain. ☐ ☐
15. Sir Simon gave Virginia a small box with jewels. ☐ ☐
16. Mr Otis wanted to give the jewels back to Lord Canterville. ☐ ☐
17. No one came to Sir Simon's funeral. ☐ ☐
18. Virginia never told Cecil her secret. ☐ ☐

2 WHO WAS IT?

Read the description and match it with the character. You can use the same character more than once.

1. ☐ She liked to paint.
2. ☐ She worked as a housekeeper.
3. ☐ He was a rich and important man.
4. ☐ They played tricks on the ghost.
5. ☐ She was a strong and healthy woman.
6. ☐ He was in love with Virginia.

7	☐	He was the oldest son of the Otis family.
8	☐	He killed his wife in 1575.
9	☐	She saw the writing on the library window many times.
10	☐	He was very tired because he could not sleep.
11	☐	They made a very frightening ghost.
12	☐	She decided to help the ghost.
13	☐	He gave Virginia a small box with jewels.
14	☐	He told Mr Otis that the house was haunted.
15	☐	He stole Virginia's paints.
16	☐	He cleaned the bloodstain in the library with 'Pinkerton's Champion Cleaner'.

A Mrs Otis
B Lord Canterville
C Sir Simon
D Virginia
E The twins

F Mrs Umney
G Mr Otis
H Washington
I Cecil

What was your favourite part of the story and why?

....

....

Who was your favourite character and why?

....

....

3 PICTURES FROM THE STORY

Look at the three pictures from the story and write your own caption under each one.

....

....

This reader uses the **EXPANSIVE READING** approach, where the text becomes a springboard to improve language skills and to explore historical background, cultural connections and other topics suggested by the text.

The new structures introduced in this step of our **GREEN APPLE** series are listed below.

Naturally, structures from lower steps are included too. For a complete list of structures used over all the three steps, see *The Black Cat Guide to Graded Readers*, which is also downloadable at no cost from our website, blackcat-cideb.com.

The vocabulary used at each step is carefully checked against vocabulary lists used for internationally recognised examinations.

 Step 1 A2

All the structures used in the previous step, plus the following:

Verb tenses
Past Simple
Past Continuous
Future reference: *will*

Verb forms and patterns
Regular and common irregular verbs
Passive forms: Present Simple and Past Simple with very common verbs
    (e.g. *made, called, born*)
Gerunds (verb + *-ing*) after some prepositions (e.g. *before, after*)

Modal verbs
Could: ability; requests
Will: future reference; offers; promises; predictions
May (present and future reference): possibility
Mustn't: prohibition
Have (got) to: external obligation

Types of clause
Subordination after *if* (zero and 1st conditionals)
Defining relative clauses with: *who, where*

Other
Comparative and superlative of adjectives (regular and irregular)
Formation of adverbs (regular and irregular)